Poems in a Nut Shell

Priscilla Mileski

Presentation by *BookLeaf Publishing*

Web: www.bookleafpub.com

E-mail: info@bookleafpub.com

ISBN: 9789360949570

First edition 2024

For my grandson, Jax

ACKNOWLEDGEMENT

A big thank you to those who have encouraged me. You know who you are. Thanks to my editor, Madeline Elizabeth Mileski.

PREFACE

The best part of the day is puttering in the garden.

Willow Slips

Willow slips cut
from a neighbor's tree
weave into a fine tight wreath.
Embellish with green satin ribbon
and magnolia leaves.

My front door welcomes
those who will step through the portal
of branches, leaves, pods and seeds.

Whoosh!

The sound of a thousand
blackbirds lifting
from the trees in a
bramble-edged clearing
in the stillness of the wood.

They rise to the skies
wave after wave, inking
the clear blue February dome.
They shout their return over
and over to forest and field
and I applaud.

Finch in a Teapot

Mr. Zebra Finch
escaped from the aviary
and hung about the garden
eating with the wild birds and
loudly lamenting the separation
from his lady of love.

After three weeks,
hopes of rescue and reunification
dimmed, persistence and patience
fell to the ground with the Spring rain.

At last he began to build a nest
in the discarded blue teapot
hanging in the garden.
His plan apparently,
to woo her from her home,
to join him in the wild.

I waited and at dusk
quickly flung a grab of fabric
over the teapot.
He scrabbled and cursed.

Safe inside they sit side by side
to preen one another and murmur soft seductive
songs.

Pussy Willow in the Spring

Pussy willow in the Spring,
gray furry kitten gnomes
alternating your way
up the branch.
You have crept so tall
year upon year
that I can no longer reach
but one low branch to cut
and bring inside.
I adore you yet again.

Hostas

Emerging from the mud,
palms up,
variegated hearts worship the rain.

Droplets
slide
down
measuring
the
vein.

Frog

I sit at my desk editing a poem
and I hear the first familiar
Spring song of the little frog
who lives beneath the pond.

He is outside my window
but sounds as though he is
sitting his muse self
in the chair beside me.

He schools me in the art of celebrating Spring.

Tree Frog Tree House

A small brown tree frog
sits in the opening
of the old wren house.
He surveys the yard.
He sings his love songs
with an audience
of sparrows and squirrels.

Be wary, be safe -
black snake
is curled in his dark cloak
in the rocks below.

Leaving the Stream

Yellow leaves drop
into the stream
to become tiny wooden boats.

Some float north with the current,
others canoe south
on a wisp of autumn breeze.

All ride the rise and fall
of an estuary
coastal tide.

The Gate Not Taken

It's late September
and the hyacinth bean
has decided now is the time
to run itself not only
on the sturdy arbor,
but across the gate,
through the latch ring,
onto the forsythia,
into the weigela,
up, up to the low hanging branch
of old mother maple.

Next year can you please
strive for more purple velvet beans
and less running around?
You are lovely but
I can't get through the gate.

Mother Earth Day

Two redbuds
and a dogwood,
bare-root and thin,
enter the garden.
Red and yellow Columbine
and Phlox paniculata
settle in between the rocks.

On knees, in fresh dug dirt,
planting is a prayer.

Moon Cast on the 2024 Eclipse

Magnolia leaves
cast crescent moons
across the pavement.

The moon-leaves flutter
and dance, lifting
your dark mood from the shadows.

They cast their own ecliptic spell upon you.

Winter Mint

Enjoying the mint I grew last summer.
Enjoying the mint so much
that I went against
all dire predictions
and planted it in my back yard.

Go ahead,
spread your carpet of wealth.
I can drink a lot of tea.

Luna Moth

Luna moth
mates only in moonlight
after midnight. She bewitches bats
with her luminous dance
and lives but a week
at the height of her beauty.
She is drawn to a light I carry
but cannot see.

Camp

Paddles pause and drip.
Slick black turtles
bask on rotted trees,
then slip into the lake
taking our held breath
deep beneath the green.

We laugh into the campfire,
our lives, our dramatic,
traumatic,
hysterically funny lives
laid open to
the pine trees above.

The Leap Day Full Moon
Low Tide

Leap day, full moon, low tide
brings out the hungry
fox who lives in the underbrush
of a tidal wetland spit.

His little-feet tracks
roam from mussel shell
to fish bone that lie stranded
on the nutrient rich sand.

The gulls feed too,
their spiky bird footprints
crisscross tiny dunes
beneath receding waves.

The moon sets the table.

Beads on a Garden Gate

Squirrels live
in the bounteous walnut tree
behind the library.

They sit, hunched little monks,
to carve the shells
with sharp teeth. They make

walnut beads for me to string
and hang along the garden gate.

Acorns with Hats

The burr oak acorn
wears a frilled
hat cap that
doubles as a nest
as it rests on the woodland floor.

In a mast year,
after the deer and squirrel
have had their fill,
I bring some home
to grace my favorite windowsill.

First Encounter

The young cottontail
saunters up the sidewalk
and pauses right in front of me.

For more than a minute
he considers me and I him.

Finally, satisfied I am only a ghost,
he moves on to nibble the chickweed.

House Sparrow

House sparrow,
you find my yard most appealing.

The filling of the feeders
happens daily,
the bathing pools
have bubblers.
Cats are deterred with much fuss
by two determined yard-dogs.
There are abundant shrubs to inspect
for the branched architectural
underpinnings of your nest.

Your happy chorus of chatter and song
rock the arborvitaes.
House sparrow, small and brown,
welcome.

Ferry Point Beach

Between two
narrow spits of pine and sand,
phragmites wave.
Oyster shells toss
back and forth
juggling the high tide
and the low.
Everything moves along that
sunny smile of beach.

Web

In a dream
I open my hand
to reveal a large brown spider.

The shock rockets me awake.
Do I weave the web
or does the web weave me?